# 50 ♥ MEET YOUR LOVER

*Laurie Rozakis*

**Macmillan**

First Edition

Copyright (c) 1997 by Laurie Rozakis
All rights reserved, including the right of
reproduction in whole or in part in any form.

Macmillan General Reference
A Simon & Schuster Macmillan Company
1633 Broadway
New York, NY 10019-6785

An Arco Book

ARCO, MACMILLAN and colophons are registered
trademarks of Simon & Schuster Inc.
Manufactured in the United States of America

10 9 8 7 6 5 4 3 2 1

ISBN: 0-02-861520-4

Book design by Scott Meola
Cover design by Amy Peppler Adams—designLab, Seattle

To my friends at CTY:
    Kara, Nora, Deanna, Jim, Jamie, Tim, Al, Gwydion, Andrew, Lee,
    Sue, and Bobro (of course).
Thanks for your help.

# INTRODUCTION

Half of all American adults are single, according to the U.S. Census Bureau. That's more than 68 million singles who are hoping to meet the right person. Single women are especially pessimistic about meeting the right mate. Many complain that all the men in America are either married, gay, or dead. Without an ark or resident matchmaker, the job of pairing up the world's singles is a daunting one.

But it's not as daunting as you might think. Let's look at those numbers another way. There are 5.7 billion people on Earth. Out of that number, 50,000 are possible Mr. or Ms. Right. That's a lot of possibles.

And that's what this book is all about. We can't guarantee that you'll meet your Dream Lover, but we *can* point you in the right directions. And remember: Thejourney can be as much fun as the destination!

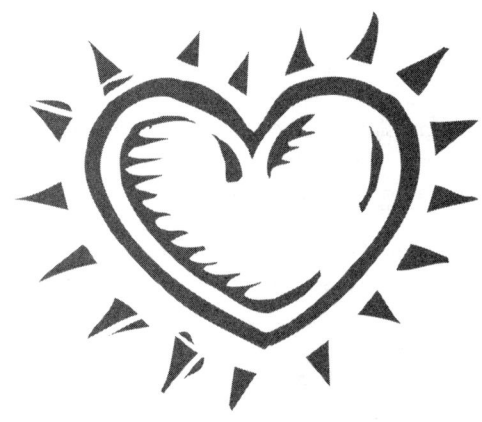

In its famous cover story on June 2, 1986, *Newsweek* magazine claimed that if you're a 30-year-old, college-educated, single woman who has never been married, you have only a 20 percent chance of finding a husband—never mind a charming one. If a woman reaches age 35 without a hubby, her chances drop to 5 percent. Age 40 and no man? According to *Newsweek*, you have a greater chance of being killed by terrorists or being struck by lightning seven times than you do of finding a husband. *Newsweek* based its article on a study conducted by professors at Harvard and Yale universities. But fortunately for singles everywhere, the U.S. Census Bureau has since discredited the researchers' findings.

One of the best ways to find a lover? Start by ignoring all the scare stories in the media about the shortage of eligible mates.

way #1

ignore the pundits

way #2

be realistic

Most men dream about falling in love with the Prom Queen; for women, it's Prince Charming in his shiny Beemer. But the real world seldom matches the dream. All women are not model-slim, pretty, and young. In fact, such women are relatively rare. On average, women have 33 percent more body fat than men. It's just part of the standard female equipment. Beauty is in the eye of the beholder and youth can be an illusion.

Likewise, all men are not slightly older, taller, and richer than their women. Check out these stats:

- The average American woman chooses a man two to four years older than she is. Since men meet their maker seven years before women (on average), the older a woman becomes, the fewer men there are for her to meet. It's obvious that if single women continue to seek out older men, their chances of finding a mate will go down, down, down. . . .

## Way #2

- And tall? How many American men do you think are six feet tall? Fewer than 10 percent! What does this mean for the dating scene? Women who are five feet six inches or taller will have a harder time finding a man they can look up to—especially if the woman wears high heels.

- Looking for Daddy Warbucks? While women still earn about 75 cents for every dollar a man earns, successful professional women can often out-earn their men. They can quite literally price themselves out of the marriage market.

The moral of the story? There are plenty of men and women out there, ripe for the picking. Just be realistic in your expectations.

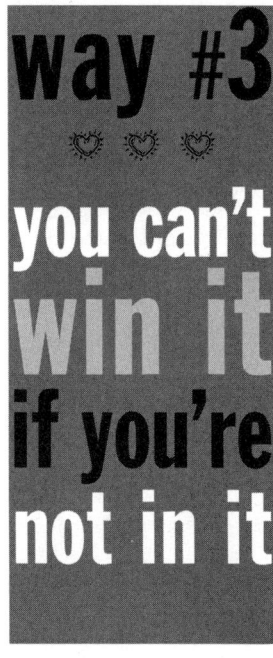

## way #3
## you can't win it if you're not in it

Woody Allen once said that 90 percent of success is showing up.

You can't score if you're not playing the field. But it's so comfortable in my house, you say. It's free and familiar. There's only one problem with staying home—you'll never meet anyone new.

So get out of the house. Hoist yourself out of the recliner and go to places with signs of life: a picnic in the park, a trendy new coffee bar, a local university. Don't go to any place where you have no chance of meeting the kind of lover you seek. Don't make your quarry do all the work.

There are millions of wonderful single people in the world, but the odds that Mr. or Ms. Right is going to knock on your door are pretty slim. You're going to have to go out of your way to find that Perfect One. You've got to be committed to the adventure. There will be plenty of hard

## Way # 3

work and not a little frustration. But in the end it will all be worth the effort. The reward? Love, desire, and passion. Sounds like common sense, and it is.

How often should you get out of the house to meet new people? That depends on your timetable. If you're willing to sit around waiting for love for 10 years, you've got plenty of time. But if you want to meet that someone special a little sooner, remember that the more you go out, the more apt you are to meet someone. It's not enough to just read this book—you have to take action! Read on to find out how.

## way #4
## make a plan

Going out aimlessly just won't do; you need a plan. Start by thinking about where you can meet people you would like to date. Review your current social opportunities by completing the diagram on the following page. In each circle, write in the name of all possible love interests. Put a + next to any names that seem especially promising.

**Way # 4**

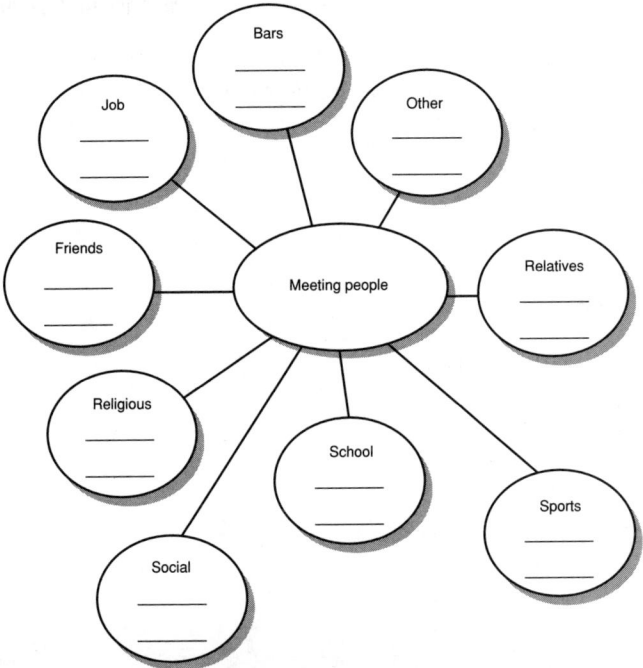

Total up the names. Which places had the most people who seemed right for you? These places will be the most promising. Read on to find out how you can build on your social network to meet more people who are right for you.

- Carol and Arnie met when I fixed them up, more than 20 years ago. Carol and I had gone to high school together; I met Arnie in college. I knew they would be good for each other, and I was right. To date, they're married nearly a quarter of a century.

- Ed and Louise got together through their mutual friend Bob. Old Bob talked about his good buddy Ed so much that Louise finally said, "So introduce me to this wonder already." The rest is history.

- Harvey thought Stephan and Joi would be a good match. Harvey was right. Today, Stephan and Joi have two adorable little girls and a good life.

The number one way to meet people in America is through mutual friends. How can you make this fact work for you? Spread the word that you're on the lookout for a suitable mate.

way #5

a friend in need is a friend indeed

Ask your friends to introduce you to their friends, relatives, and coworkers. But don't leave anything to guesswork. Tell your friends exactly what kind of lover you want. Be as specific as possible: height, weight, age, career, family, education—whatever you value in a possible mate. Encourage your friends to include you in dinner parties, graduation bashes, holiday gatherings—all the places where you're likely to meet a suitable lover.

## way #6
### do your homework

Friends can be great sources for meeting new love interests, but proceed with caution. Would you hire someone for a job without an interview? Of course not. Likewise, when looking for love, you should be reasonably informed about any possibilities. Say a friend mentions a great new coworker. Based on a superficial description, you think: "Sounds just right for me." Think again before you act. Have your friend do a complete check. Include:

- Age
- Occupation
- Sexual preference
- Romantic history
- Health
- Family

Says a single woman named Lucy: "I won't let a friend set me up with a guy unless she's met him first—otherwise, you never know what will show up at the door." Words to the wise.

# 50 WAYS TO MEET YOUR LOVER

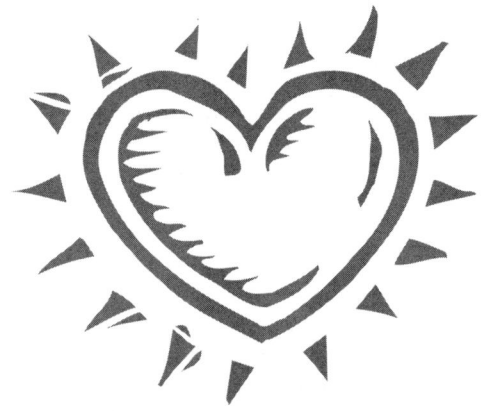

## way #7 ♥ ♥ ♥ career choice

**M**ost people select a job based on such factors as salary, status, enjoyment, and commute. Nothing wrong with these criteria, but consider adding one more factor to the equation: love.

According to a study of 3,000 singles conducted by researchers Simenauer and Carroll, about 10 percent of all love affairs begin between people who meet each other on the job (*The New Americans*. New York: Simon and Schuster, 1982). In another more recent survey, about 2,000 career women claimed that a romance between colleagues is four times more likely to last than a romance between people who meet outside the workplace. Informal estimates conclude that about 20 percent of on-the-job love affairs lead to marriage.

Meeting a lover on the job is not without risks, however. Most important, what happens if the romance doesn't pan out? Will one of you be looking for a new job? The danger is not as extreme as you might have been led

to believe. Fewer than 5 percent of the workers in this situation felt that their love affair had hurt their career.

The moral of the story: If it suits your talents and training, choose a job where you are dealing with many people daily. Or choose an office where there are lots of single people.

It's not just meeting a lover—it's meeting the *right* kind of lover. If career is your turn-on, try hunting in these places:

- Promised Mom and Dad you'd come home with a doctor? Check out Seattle, home to the highest concentration of M.D.s in any city. Next come San Francisco, California, and Boston, Massachusetts.

- Looking for a lover who is good with bits and bytes? The biggest concentrations of computer scientists are in San Jose, California; Seattle, Washington; and Austin, Texas.

- How about a life with a lawyer? Go shopping for love in Washington, D.C.; San Francisco; and Seattle.

- Athletes are in abundance in Austin; San Diego, California; and Honolulu, Hawaii.

way #8

choice careers

- San Francisco, Seattle, and New York are the "in" places for artists.
- If music's your thing, it's Nashville, Los Angeles, and San Francisco for you.

**C**onsider volunteer work. There are virtually countless opportunities to help others and make your community a better place in which to live. Look in the telephone book, local community directory, or newspaper to find out how you can pitch in. Along with contributing to society, you'll also increase your visibility in the community and meet new friends. New friends with whom you can find a new life. New friends who can bring you love. New friends who are apt to be generous and community-minded. Here are some ideas to get you started volunteering:

- Rotary International
- Lions International
- Your local school board
- Historical societies
- Condo shareholder groups
- Youth boards

- The Parent-Teacher Associations
- Your local library board
- Civic associations
- Garden clubs
- Senior citizens' groups
- Blood donation

Remember, there are scores of ways you can volunteer—and meet that special someone.

"Whatever you do, don't talk to strangers!"

Mommy always told us to stay away from strangers, and that was good advice when we were in elementary school. But we're all grown up now. There's no denying that strangers can be dangerous. But it's also true that strangers can become friends. If you don't meet a lover through a friend or on the job, odds are that your next lover is a stranger to you now. As a result, if you want to meet that ideal person, you're going to have to set aside what you learned about talking to strangers.

You'll have the greatest chance of meeting someone new at a gathering full of strangers. For the purposes of finding a new love, the perfect party would be one where no one knows anyone else. That way you are all forced to meet and mingle.

way #10

strange encounters

If you're like most of us, you spend the greatest part of your day with people you already know—at work and after hours. It's comfortable and safe, but you're not going to meet anyone new.

> **Remember: There are no strangers, only friends we haven't met yet.**

Allison always goes trolling for single men with her buddy Christi. Even though Christi has a lover, she accompanies Allison on her forays. Two women are less threatening to a man than one; two men are less threatening to a woman than one. A woman traveling with another woman is more likely than a lone woman to entertain the overtures of a strange male. Any person traveling as part of a pair also seems more solid and reliable than a solo act: Hey, at least you know that she/he has *one* friend.

Further advantages:

- There's safety in numbers.
- You'll usually have a fine time even if you don't hit pay dirt.

So travel with a buddy.

way #11

the buddy system

**CAUTION:** Your buddy must be of the same sex. Otherwise, potential lovers will assume that you're already attached.

**N**ow that you've met a few dozen strangers, it's time to get down to business. Take a deep breath, look the person straight in the eye, and ... get involved in some trivial conversation. Talk about something shallow and superficial. Yes, you heard right—talk about the weather, the president's jogging, the high price of gasoline. Start with something prosaic and relaxing to put people at ease.

This is not the time to go into your pet theory of supply-side economics or explain the intricacies of nuclear fission. Keep it simple and easy. You'll put the other person—and yourself—at ease.

way #12

can we talk?

## way #13
## can we really talk?

OK, you've broken the ice with some small talk, nothing flashy. Now it's time to get down and dirty. Start asking some personal questions to find out what you need to know—before you get stuck with someone you don't want to be stuck with.

It's worth the risk to find out what you need to know *now*, before you invest your emotions, time, and money. Think about spending six months buying that beautiful woman champagne only to discover that she is on parole for assaulting her schnauzer. How about wasting a year of your time before you find out that your hunka burning love is saddled with alimony payments that exceed the GNP of a small banana republic?

Now is the time to pry. You can reveal what you want—or need—to find out the lowdown. For example, you can say, "My last relationship lasted two years but ended badly. How about yours?"

## way #14
### where the boys (and girls) are

If you want to meet someone of the opposite sex (or the sex you prefer), you have to go where they are. This is not a tricky concept. Unfortunately, most people feel most comfortable with people of their own sex. Despite all the hoopla about women's liberation and men's liberation and everyone-else's-liberation, men and women are still doing "men" and "women" things. Yes, we have read all the articles in news magazines about role reversals, but the majority of men are still most comfortable tinkering with traditional men stuff like cars and plumbing, and most women are still doing the laundry, cooking, and shopping (whether they want to or not). Test it yourself. Visit an auto repair shop or a nail salon and see who is buying the carburetor and who is getting the leg wax.

The result? Most of the time, the sexes don't mingle unless someone makes a deliberate effort.

If you want to meet a woman, ask yourself, "Where do women spend their time?" If you want to meet a man, ask

yourself, "Where do men spend their time?" Then resolve to go to the places on your list. For example, if you want to meet a woman, try folk dancing, aerobics classes, or the women's racks in a department store. Want to meet a man? Try a boxing match or a boat show.

**way #15**

❥ ❥ ❥

**road map to romance**

**M**en and women are everywhere—but there are more of them in large cities. This is simple logic. More people = more dateable people. (We'll get to the surplus of men in Greenland and the United Arab Emirates later.) "In New York, where I live," said one woman, "you walk down the street and see maybe 20 good-looking guys. They smile, you smile. It's like everyone is an option. How do you pick? You don't; you date them all." No doubt our speaker is a buff 20-year-old model who has the right to be overly optimistic, but there is no denying that many cities are more fertile hunting grounds for dates than most suburbs and farm areas.

Here's how the major cities stack up, based on their male/female ratio of twentysomethings. If you prefer older dates, go for the cities with the fewest twentysomethings.

| City | Number of 20ish men per 100 20ish women | % of population consisting of people in their 20s |
| --- | --- | --- |
| Anchorage, AL | 108 | 18 |
| Austin, TX | 107 | 25 |
| Baltimore, MD | 92 | 18 |
| Boston, MA | 99 | 26 |
| Chicago, IL | 99 | 18 |
| Cleveland, OH | 91 | 18 |
| Columbus, OH | 101 | 24 |
| Dallas, TX | 107 | 21 |
| Detroit, MI | 84 | 16 |
| El Paso, TX | 95 | 17 |
| Jacksonville, FL | 109 | 18 |

| Honolulu, HI | 106 | 16 |
| --- | --- | --- |
| Houston, TX | 106 | 19 |
| Indianapolis, IN | 91 | 18 |
| Los Angeles, CA | 116 | 21 |
| Memphis, TN | 94 | 17 |
| Milwaukee, WI | 85 | 18 |
| Nashville, TN | 94 | 19 |
| New York, NY | 94 | 17 |
| Philadelphia, PA | 97 | 18 |
| Phoenix, AZ | 105 | 18 |
| San Antonio, TX | 98 | 18 |
| San Diego, CA | 124 | 22 |
| San Francisco, CA | 104 | 19 |

(continued)

| City | Number of 20ish men per 100 20ish women | % of population consisting of people in their 20s |
|---|---|---|
| San Jose, CA | 114 | 19 |
| Seattle, WA | 104 | 20 |
| Washington, DC | 90 | 20 |
| **U.S. Average** | **102** | **16** |

🖤 🖤 🖤 🖤 🖤 🖤 🖤 🖤 🖤 🖤 🖤 🖤 🖤 🖤 🖤 🖤 🖤 🖤 🖤 🖤 🖤 🖤 🖤 🖤 🖤 🖤

**way #16**

🖤 🖤 🖤

**small town lover**

Let's focus on the ladies for a moment. Just because a large city has men doesn't mean that they're your kind of men. The reason that California has so many men is that it has 100,000 prison inmates—the largest number of any state. Many of these guys are single, but they're usually not available for a night on the town. And in some cities—such as San Francisco—the men who aren't in prison are likely to be more interested in having dinner with each other than with a woman.

San Diego? Most of the men are in the service. Nashville? Many are struggling musicians waiting to be discovered. And unless you're a Gen X rep, stay out of Boston—too many college boys, not enough men.

Yes, there are more single people in large cities, but good things don't always come in big packages. Here are five smaller American cities that are great places to hunt for a man.

| City | Number of men for every 100 women |
|---|---|
| Ames, IA | 111.3 |
| Rapid City, SD | 98.7 |
| Cheyenne, WY | 97.2 |
| Missoula, MT | 96.8 |
| Fargo, ND | 95.7 |

## way #17

### location, location, location

Women, if the percentage of men in cities gets you down, there's still another route: Look out of the United States. The Arab states, for example, are chock-full of men. Check out these numbers:

| United Arab Emirates | 68.9% male |
| Qatar | 63.6% male |
| Kuwait | 59.6% male |
| Bahrain | 58.4% male |
| And there's always Greenland | It's 54.3% male. |

Or read on for more.

**50 WAYS TO MEET YOUR LOVER**

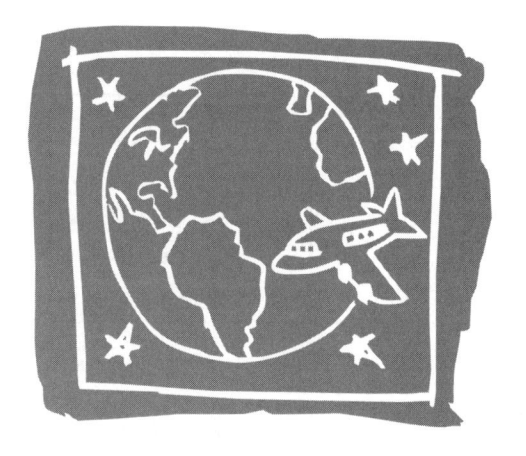

## way #18
♡ ♡ ♡
## see the world and fall in love

Jimmy and Marie met in Jerusalem in 1994 on a hot, muddy summer day. They were both teachers on an educational tour through the Holy Land. Jimmy came from Meadville, Pennsylvania, and Marie from San Francisco. They hit it off right away and spent the week together touring schools and taking in the sights. It was not love at first sight, but they did exchange a few letters after returning to the United States. The following Labor Day weekend, when Marie went to visit Jimmy, the couple knew they had found love.

> **Travel broadens the soul as well as the mind. It can also do wonders for your love life.**

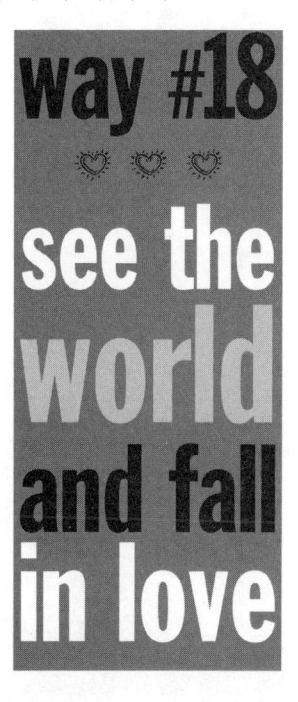

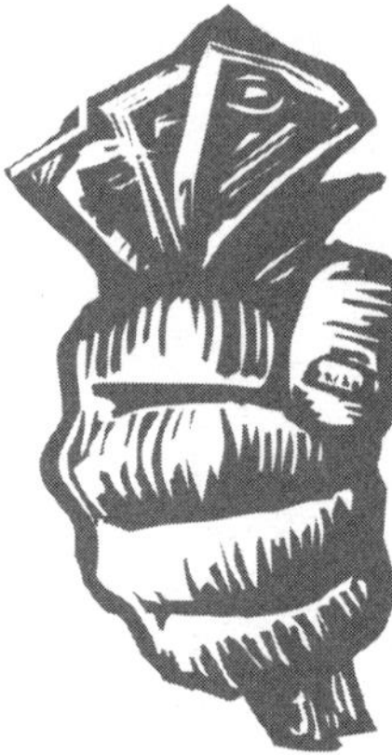

Looking for bucks? Is money your turn-on? You're most likely to meet a millionaire in the following states. They are arranged in alphabetical order:

> Alaska
>
> California
>
> Connecticut
>
> Delaware
>
> Florida
>
> Hawaii
>
> Maine
>
> Maryland
>
> Massachusetts
>
> Nevada
>
> New Hampshire

way #19

marry a millionaire

New Jersey

New York

North Dakota

Rhode Island

Wyoming

We promised you the lowdown on Alaska, and here it is. Women, if you're thinking of packing your bags and heading north, you've been in the sun too long. It's likely that you're imagining Alaska's men are rugged, romantic hunks who come equipped with a pair of snowshoes, kayak, and fur parka. Think again.

According to Alaskan women, you're much more likely to encounter a man who has gone to great lengths to put as much distance between himself and his past as possible. As one Alaskan woman says, "The odds may be great—but the goods are odd." She has since moved out of Alaska.

People in the lower 48 tend to think that Alaskan men are like tomatoes in August: theirs for the picking. Yes, there are many, but those veggies may not be choice. There's often a good reason why these men aren't married. No doubt some came looking for adventure. But others came because they needed jobs that did not require much in the way of schooling or skills.

**way #20**

**(half) baked Alaska**

And while there are more men than women in Alaska, there just aren't that many people. Anchorage, the state's largest city, has only 133 people per square mile—as compared to 12,000 per square mile in Boston. If you think you'll love Alaska, give it a try. But go for the solitude or scenery—not the men.

## way #21
## take the bull by the horns

It's Friday night. Michael and Richard hit the hottest pick-up place in town: the superbookstore-cum-coffeeshop. What do they do upon arrival? They head straight for the Renaissance Drama section and plant themselves so firmly in the corner that no man, woman, or child could find them unless they were looking for a place to stash the contents of Fort Knox.

It's not enough to hit the places where the elite meet to mingle. Be assertive. Walk up to someone who looks interesting. Speak. Get into the person's line of vision. This can backfire only if there is an outstanding warrant for your arrest and the person is later called to give a detailed description of you. The great tragedy of single life is that 99 percent of the time, when we see people we're attracted to, we don't put ourselves in a comfortable position so that a conversation can begin.

Break out of the rut. Be part of the one percent. Go with a simple opening line like "Hi" and strike up a

conversation. You'll still have time to run the FBI check before the first date.

## way #22
### ♥ ♥ ♥
# hit the singles bars

Some people go to bookstores to meet people, but most people go to bookstores to buy books. Singles bars, on the other hand, exist precisely so single people have a place to go where it is hard to hear what anyone says and everyone's judgment is impaired.

Wade into the human crush, buy something nonalcoholic to drink, and get ready to start a conversation. Make an odd comment that deserves a reply. Avoid clever repartee. Clever openings usually sound slick. That's a real turn-off. Conversation is an incremental process. Start with something innocuous about the weather, for example. The other person replies and you keep chatting until you find a mutually agreeable topic. Still in a panic? Try . . .

Five never-fail conversation topics:

- Food
- The trial du jour
- Inexpensive vacation spots

- Outlandish home remedies for the common cold
- Uplifting tales of how a friend found an unbeatable parking spot

If you're still at a loss for words, prepare by reading some of the latest bestsellers, going to the hot movies, and scanning the supermarket tabloids for the latest wicked scandal.

***Note:*** *If you meet someone in a bar and give out your phone number, how long should you realistically wait before giving up hope? Assuming you met the person over the weekend, Wednesday is a reasonable target date. If you don't hear by then, it's not terribly likely that you will. The best way to avoid this whole game, of course, is to take the person's number and do the calling yourself.*

## way #23
### 🤍 🤍 🤍
# mother knows best

Visualize this scene: You've just gotten your first real job and it's time to sign the apartment lease. Mom and Dad have decided to come along to "help." Help? At the rental office, there's a person of the opposite sex getting ready to sign a lease. This person is about your age and is so suitable that he might as well have "MARRIAGEABLE" written across his forehead. You stare hard at your mother, sending psychic waves of "No! Don't do it! Don't ask him! Please!"

Naturally, your mother asks, "So, are you single?" He is. Ditto with the next two men who walk into the office, whom she also accosts. This puts Mom in a real pickle: Which man is the right one for her darling? When she makes her choice, she simply gives the lucky winner the address of your new apartment. Then she adds, "If you need any more information, just call me," and gives the young man *her* home number. After all, you don't have a phone yet.

Annoying, yes—but also exceedingly useful. Mr. Real Estate might not be Mr. Right, but his best friend, brother, or coworker might be. Don't be so quick to squelch Mom. She may be on the right track.

## way #24

### 🖤 🖤 🖤

## say cheese!

Here's another Mom method for helping her child meet The One.

Every six months, Debbie's mother takes a roll of photos of Debbie, so that she always has new snapshots to show to friends and acquaintances who have eligible sons. Debbie hates the idea, but then again, maybe one of these guys is worth meeting. So every six months, Debbie and Mom have the same fight.

Debbie says that she will pose for the pictures if her mother will give her final say over which ones she shows. Mother always assures Debbie that her wishes will be honored. But somehow, when the pictures are finally developed, Mom refuses to let Debbie see them. Mom insists that only a mother can tell when her daughter is being shown to her best advantage.

Again, don't be so quick to take Mom's camera away. She may be on to something good!

Audrey's parents were both studying in a library at a large Midwestern university 20 years ago. They were single and had not yet met each other. It was late, and there was a full moon. Each thought the library was empty. Audrey's mother, at one end of the library, went to the window and started to howl at the moon. Audrey's father, who was at the other end of the library, also started to howl at the moon. When Audrey's mother heard somebody else howling, she walked to where the sound was coming from and saw a young man standing in front of an open window.

Audrey's mother realized that she had seen this young man on the campus, but she had always thought he seemed sort of "nerdy." When she saw him howling, her opinion changed.

They talked for a while. She hoped he would ask her out, but he didn't, so she asked him. He was quite shy, but

**way #25**

**howl at the moon**

she was very fond of him and hung in there for five long years. Finally, he proposed, and they got married.

So howl at the moon or do something equally free-spirited. Maybe you'll meet a free spirit like your own.

**M**e: Handsome, romantic executive. *You:* educated, bright, very pretty SWF, 40–49. As soul mates, we will find romance and adventure.

## YOU NEVER KNOW

Trusting, well-built, sensitive SWJM enjoys bridge, dancing, and workouts. Seeks attractive woman 25–35 for a lasting relationship.

## CRAZY WAY TO MEET

Blue-eyed lady loves romance, music, tennis, dining. Seeking honest, good-looking lifetime buddy.

---

**way #26**

**it pays to advertise**

A surprising number of people have met their mates through the personal ads. More than two million personal ads run each year. According to conservative estimates, more than 10,000 people a year who meet through the personal ads get married.

If you do decide to place an ad, check the abbreviations to make sure you understand the lingo. Here are some of the most commonly used abbreviations:

| S = single | D = divorced | C = Christian | J = Jewish |
| --- | --- | --- | --- |
| M = male | F = female | G = gay | N/S = nonsmoker |
| B = black | A = Asian | W = white | P = professional |

Make your ad short and snappy. Don't lie, but make the most of your best!

# way #27

## blind dates

For some reason, the blind date has always been snickered at. It seems that everyone has a horror story about a blind date they, a friend, or a relative endured. So dreadful! So embarrassing! Agony! There *is* a risk involved in a blind date—but if you never take a chance, you can never win. Think of a blind date this way:

> Once upon a time there was a poor man who struggled to support his wife and 10 children. His wife was ill; his children were demanding. The man was religious and prayed to God every day. Surely God would provide. But one day, the man reached the end of his patience, and he rebuked God: "Dear God, I have been a faithful, religious man. I pray every day. I help the few people who are less fortunate. I give to charity; I do good works. Would it be so terrible if you helped me just a little? Couldn't you see to it that I win even a small lottery?"

> *A beam of light flashed from the sky, parting the clouds, and God replied, "Couldn't you at least buy a lottery ticket?"*

In the lottery of love, you should at least buy a ticket. So the next time you get the chance to go on a blind date, do it.

**way #28**

♡ ♡ ♡

**the life you save may be your wife's**

In 1991, Heather Schmidt accepted a position as a substitute teacher at a Long Island elementary school. That October, she suddenly began choking on a lollipop that had lodged in her throat. Frantically, the secretary called the emergency squad. Mark Rosenberg and his assistant came to Heather's rescue. They put her on a stretcher and took her to the hospital. The doctors and nurses took care of her and she recovered quickly with only minor discomfort. That night, Mark came back to check on Heather. Heather never met him; she only knew his voice.

Two years later to the exact date, a mutual friend introduced them. At first, Mark didn't realize their paths had crossed earlier, but when he saw Heather, he remembered her face. Although Mark was handsome and charming, Heather wanted nothing to do with him because she already had a boyfriend. Mark, in contrast, knew this was the girl he was going to marry. The mutual friend pressed Heather; Mark called the next day. It was not until the

third conversation that Heather realized Mark had been the one who saved her life. They talked, they dated, they fell in love.

On May 27, 1995, Mark and Heather were married. A lollipop was attached to each favor that they gave out at the wedding.

We're *not* suggesting that rescue squad workers troll the stretchers for possible dates, or that people subject themselves to injuries to meet handsome EMTs. We *are* suggesting that you explore unusual as well as usual avenues to meet people. Take another look at the mail carrier, and don't be so quick to dismiss that attractive server at your local coffee shop.

## way #29
### 🜲 🜲 🜲
## nearer my God to thee

Actor Chazz Palminteri got his big break when Robert De Niro showed up at his one-man play *A Bronx Tale*. This led the 43-year-old Bronx native to a role in Woody Allen's *Bullets Over Broadway*—and an Academy Award nomination. Since then, Palminteri has been busy shuttling between Hollywood and Broadway. Along the way, he found time to meet his mate.

They met in church. To be exact, he met her coming out of church. Their meeting took place in Los Angeles at St. Charles Church, right off Lancasham in the Valley. Mass was over. She was coming out. Their eyes met. Chazz wanted to say something to her, but the priest was there. What was he going to say, "Father, can I borrow a pen? I want to get this girl's number?" So he didn't say anything and she kept walking. The next week, he went to a nightclub and she was there with her friends. He looked at her and she looked at him. They didn't go to church together right away, but it wasn't long before they were married. And they've been together ever since.

We recommend religious services as a venue for connecting with the opposite sex. Among the advantages are knowing that the person shares your values and likely much of your background.

## way #30
## lunch 'n love

**G**uy meets girl at the corner deli. He falls madly in love. She gets a beard burn on the first date. "We were kissing and kissing and kissing," she said. They parted after three weeks—he had a crazy notion of flying her to Cuba—and she returned to her boyfriend, with whom she had a child. He settled down with other women. But every so often the former lovers would call each other up and tease, "Do you still want to marry me?" The last time she phoned, he said yes, and two weeks later they were married. "I was ready to make that official commitment," he said. "I knew it was time."

This is how actor Nicolas Cage met his wife, actress Patricia Arquette. They bonded over the salami at Canter's delicatessen in Los Angeles. The two dated briefly, then stayed in occasional telephone contact until they came together again (at Canter's) a few months before their wedding.

The moral of the story? Pay more attention to the people at your corner deli while you're ordering your egg salad on rye.

## way #31
## bleeding hearts

The Japanese believe that a lover's suitability can be determined by his or her blood type. Yes, you read that correctly. If you subscribe to this theory, we suggest you consider frequenting blood banks. Especially those in Japan. The four blood types are A, O, B, and AB. Here's what the Japanese believe each one signifies:

- **A** Represents "Eastern" values: Organized, follows the rules, scheduled—perhaps a bit too rigid. Most Japanese are blood type A.

- **O** Represents "American/Western" values: Creative, antiauthority, deciding one's own priorities—perhaps too obstinate.

- **B** Easygoing, sympathetic, kind.

- **AB** A combination of A and B: Organized but kind; scheduled but easy—a relaxed person.

## way #32
## the game of love

Randi and Lou met by accident in the parking lot of a public tennis court and decided to have a few quick volleys while waiting for their scheduled tennis partners to arrive. The pair found they were well matched on the court. Over the next few months, one tennis match stretched to another and another. This led to dinner, dancing, and romance. Randi and Lou found they were well matched off the tennis court, too.

Consider sports as a great way of meeting potential lovers. You'll be helping your heart in more ways than one.

Tennis, anyone?

## way #33

## row, row, row your boat

"I was on the university rowing team, and Molly came on as the coxswain," says Bob, explaining how he met his lover.

In their first conversation, Bob asked, "So, did you ever cox before?"

She replied, "I've never been in a boat before."

> **Moral: You don't even have to play the sport to meet a great mate.**

## way #34

## the anti-date

Instead of looking for a way to meet likely lovers, try the "anti-date." Anti-dating, by definition, is the practice of going to large social gatherings or events where you'll run into a person you would really like to get to know better. Have some chit-chat, but resist the urge to set up a date. Instead, check around to make sure your love interest is going to the same event. Once there, zoom in the focus. Talk, laugh, and seduce. Meander off together to a secluded corner.

After several rounds of parties, you can move to the "Let's meet for dinner at eight" stage of the relationship.

## way #35
## food for love

The best place to meet a prospective lover? The grocery store! Especially early Sunday morning. Some attractive single shoppers hit the supermarket between 7:30 and 9:00 a.m., looking for more than a jar of sauce or a pound of apples. Besides, if they are food shopping that early, you can be sure they weren't at the bars the night before.

You can also tell a great deal about a person by the food he or she buys. Cart full of fresh fruits and vegetables? There's a person seriously involved with nutrition and fitness. Cart loaded with Spam, Tang, and beef jerky? So many chemicals in that system that he'd glow in the dark. No need for a night light with this fella.

Best of all, the supermarket affords great chances for a pickup. You can chat about ingredients, foods, cooking tips. Here's our hint: Start a conversation about a recipe. Feign uncertainty about exact amounts but offer to call with the information after you get home and look it up in

## Way # 35

your cookbook. Of course, this means you will have to get his or her telephone number. The conversation might go this way:

*Scene: At the produce display, early one Sunday morning.*

**You:** "I see you're looking at the artichokes. How do you prepare them?"

**Love Interest:** "Actually, I've never made them before. What do you do with them?"

**You:** "I have a great recipe for them. You need 1 cup of bread crumbs, spices, butter, onions, and garlic. I'm not sure how much butter, though. If you give me your phone number, I'll give you a call with the exact amounts."

**Love Interest:** "555-1234."

Don't give out your phone number until you have chatted on the phone several times. And always call back to see how the recipe turned out. You may end up with a cold fish, but there's always the chance of a hot tamale.

**way #36**

**politics makes *strange* bedfellows**

We present for your consideration the case of Democrat James Carville and Republican Mary Matalin. Theirs was perhaps the most unlikely way to meet your mate. The "ragin' Cajun" Carville was the mastermind behind Bill Clinton's 1992 presidential victory; Mary Matalin was running the George Bush campaign. So here's still another way to meet your mate—work on opposing political campaigns.

And they all lived happily ever after.... When Clinton won, Matalin told Carville: "You make me sick. I hate your guts." On second thought, perhaps you'll want to keep reading for less stressful ways to find the love of your life.

## way #37
## music madness

Outdoor concerts add up to music, sun, food—and maybe even love. Lollapalooza, for example, is a single's obstacle course set to music. It's a great way to see how someone stands up to a constant assault on the senses. You'll be dirty, sweaty, and tired, but you'll also discover whether the one you eyeballed is a joiner or a loner. Considerate? Does he or she let you go into the Porta-Potty first? You'll also get the skinny on your potential's politics.

**CAUTION: Proceed with this method only if you like the music, look good in junk food, and have no major objection to body piercing and tattoos. Otherwise, you might find yourself saddled with a Deadhead or an overage refugee from Woodstock.**

**M**y father looked for likely women in the dining rooms of large resorts. One night he got more than he bargained for when he picked up a comely young woman who was destined to become his wife and my mother.

Loitering outside the dining hall, he gave my mother his standard pickup line, something about coming to see his new car. She fell for it, and together they strolled out to his shining new Buick. They got into the car, my father shifted into reverse, and surreptitiously let his free hand slip to my mother's knee. Excited beyond reason by his good fortune, my father promptly plowed the car into a tree. Six months later, they were married, and my father smashed car bumpers regularly for the next 40 years.

Looking for a mate who shares your interest in moo shoo pork and bananas flambé? Consider spending more time loitering around the dining halls of large resorts, casinos, and hotels.

## way #38

### food for thought

## way #39

## online love

One of the hottest new ways to meet a lover is through online computer matchmaking services and by surfing the net. All of the major online services such as Prodigy and America Online have singles bulletin boards and chatrooms. On AOL, for example, you can "meet" people in chatrooms such as the *Best Li'l Chatroom*, *The Breakfast Club*, *The Meeting Place*, and *The Saloon*. All it takes to hook up is a modem and a comfortable chair.

On the World Wide Web, you can try these buttons:

www.match.com

http://www.webpersonals.com

http://www.autonomy.com//luv.htm (Love and Romance Master Pages)

E-mail us with the results!

## way #40
## love and learning

One of the best places to meet singles is in school. Have you graduated from high school? Are you done with college? Then try noncredit classes offered by your local high school or community college. The Learning Annex, The Learning Exchange, the National Association of Single Persons Information Network, Cambridge Center for Adult Education, CareerTrack Seminars, Discovery Center, and other well-known institutions also sponsor personal enrichment classes throughout the United States.

A recent survey revealed that nearly half the people enrolled in noncredit classes did so to meet other people—not to gain knowledge in a specific subject area. In fact, some courses are specifically aimed at singles. They focus on ways to meet other singles and how to be content with the single life.

Want to meet women? Try classes that deal with self-improvement, psychology, relationships, and the arts. Looking for single men? Enroll in classes that focus on

investments, auto repair, home improvement, and sports. Not in the mood to skim the catalog and figure the odds? Consider approaching the registrar and asking point-blank which courses attract the most single men or single women.

## way #41

### love letters

Millions and millions of people around the world dream of starting a new life in America. But American immigration laws restrict the number of people who can enter our shores. One way to circumvent these laws is to marry an American citizen. This has resulted in scores of correspondence dating services that help American men meet foreign women. Most of these services publish directories that include descriptions and photographs of their foreign clients. American men then write to these women with the goal of setting up a match.

The services are perfectly legal—but the phony marriages that result in many cases are not. Usually these marriages end quickly, after money has changed hands. The United States Immigration Service is wise to the game.

But not all correspondence services involve American men meeting foreign women for the purpose of citizenship. There are some respectable correspondence services that help singles set up relationships through the mail. The

best advice? If you're thinking of going the letter-writing route, investigate the correspondence service carefully. If it's on the up-and-up, stock up on stamps and get a good pen.

## way #42
## where singles meet to mingle

Singles clubs may not always match you with your Ideal One, but at least they give you a chance to be in the same room. And that's a good start.

Singles clubs cover a wide range of activities and ages. Some clubs are affiliated with religious organizations; others are commercially sponsored. There are sharp differences in standards as well. Some groups are relaxed about differences in age, while others adhere strictly to the rules. And some clubs for "professionals" may have a very broad definition of "professional." Nonetheless, many people have a good time at singles clubs and some even meet their significant other through them.

Look in your telephone book or community directory for the singles clubs that meet your criteria.

**way #43**

**dance your way to love**

Listen up, twinkletoes. Dancing is a fabulous way to meet singles. It's a socially acceptable way to approach strangers and get to know them a little bit better. Dancing even provides the perfect opening line: "Would you like to dance?" You can dance at clubs, discos, bars, or anywhere the music and space allow.

There are dances for all tastes, too. If you're not comfortable with the disco scene, consider square dancing or folk dancing. Organizations across the country specialize in square-dancing events; local community centers and libraries often feature folk dancing.

Can't boogie? Got two left feet? Sign up for dance lessons at your local library, community center, or dance studio. It's another great way to meet some neat people. Just make sure you enroll in a class that is geared to singles rather than couples.

## way #44

### outdoor clubs

Dance clubs make you feel closed in? Do you prefer the great outdoors? Look for a group of singles who think the way you do. Many singles clubs cater to people who enjoy outdoor activities such as skiing, hiking, walking, bicycling, and river rafting. Possibilities range from *Loners on Wheels* (an organization of RV owners aged 50 and over) to the *Sierra Club* (an organization of outdoor enthusiasts that has singles clubs under its auspices). Check in your telephone book for more organizations that meet in your area.

What happens if you don't really like sports? We have it on good authority that up to 40 percent of the people who join some singles sports clubs do so just to meet new people!

## way #45
## single parent clubs

Are you a single parent? Then you know how difficult it can be to find a mate who shares your interests in home and family. Consider looking into a single parent club such as Parents Without Partners. PWP has more than 500 chapters throughout the United States. Members must be single parents—you're eligible for membership even if your child is 60 years old! To find out more about Parents Without Partners, look in the community bulletin board of your local newspaper or cable TV channel. PWP is also listed in the telephone book.

Other groups include Mothers Without Custody, the National Congress for Men, and Single Parent Resource Center. Check your local directory for more information on these and other single parent groups.

## way #46
## start your own club

There are clubs for singles who are vertically challenged or horizontally impaired. There are singles clubs for athletes, swingers, widows and widowers. Single minorities, single nonsmokers, and single parents have their own meeting places. Singles who earn a lot have their own clubs; singles who bowl have theirs. There is a singles club for nearly everyone. But what happens if you're one of those "*nearly* everyones" who can't find the club that fits your specific interest? Start your own singles club!

First, gather a group of your single friends. Together, scout the area for a meeting place. Possibilities include members' homes, a library, or a church or synagogue. When you're all ready to go, use the media to notify other people about your group. Post news of your group online, in the local newspaper, on the radio. Most public television and radio stations offer free public service announcements for local nonprofit groups. Finally, set up some guidelines to help people feel at ease with the group. One good way to help relax people is to serve light refreshments. Enjoy!

## way #47

### matchmaker, matchmaker, make me a match

Hate sports? Sick of classes? Exhausted your friends' friends? Consider subscribing to a dating service. While a dating service usually costs more than non-profit singles clubs, a dating service offers a more professional approach to meeting your significant someone. There are many, many dating services available, but they fall into two basic types: matchmaking services and do-it-yourself matching.

- Matchmaking dating services find a match for you. Matchmaking services may be either *computer dating services* or *personal introduction services*. With a computer dating service, first you fill out a questionnaire that describes you and your ideal mate. Then the computer matches you with possibilities from its data files. With a personal introduction service, a real live person finds a match for you. Computer dating services tend to be very reasonable; personal introduction services can run into the thousands of dollars.

- Do-it-yourself matchmaking offers different ways that you can go through the membership files yourself. Depending on the service, you can look at written profiles, photos, and videos. Be aware that information may be fudged and photos old or retouched. Video offers the most realistic look at the possible lover, but this method is the most costly of the three.

You can find the dating service that's right for your needs by reading the personal ads in newspapers and magazines. Be careful to screen the service carefully before you invest, however. Find out how long the service has been in business and how many active members they have. Check the cost, length of membership, and reputation, too. Approach shopping for a dating service as you would approach shopping for any major investment.

## way #48
### be a star

Try TV. Not watching it—being on it. Among the many intriguing new date shows is MTV's *Singled Out*. Described in a recent article as "a televised hormonal pep rally," it features contestants rooting not for a gridiron victory, but rather for the abstract concept of finding true love on a soundstage in Burbank.

If you're going to be in town during a taping, write for tickets to this show or any of the others like it. Even if you don't meet the lover of your dreams, you'll have a great time and 15 minutes of fame.

**way #49**

**three great ideas**

## Like a Fine Wine

Looking to meet someone a little older? Try "Wives of Older Men," an international networking service for folks seeking May–December romances. WOOM founder Beliza Ann Furman married a 38-year-old man when she was but 23. "There's a tremendous amount of prejudice against these couples," Furman says. "Families don't often welcome them with open arms."

## Political Action

Actor Eddie Murphy met his wife Nicole in 1988 at a lunch where Jesse Jackson was speaking. Consider supporting a political candidate as a way of helping the democratic process—and yourself.

## Way # 49

# The Play's the Thing

Neve Campbell, an actress on *Party of Five*, met her husband Jeff Colt at a Toronto theater—he was bartending, she was performing in *The Phantom of the Opera*. As this method indicates, you can find love in the theater on or off stage.

## way #50

### just do it

OK, you've met someone you are interested in; now how do you ask him/her out? That's easy. Just follow this simple three-step plan: choose how, decide what, just ask.

## Choose How

How are you going to approach the object of your desire? Generally speaking, there are two ways to communicate with a prospective lover: face-to-face or by phone. It's up to you to choose the method that suits your personal style. If you blush at personal encounters, the phone's best for you. If things go badly, you can always fake an incoming call and sever the connection.

Face-to-face is the way to go if you meet every day and phoning would be awkward and artificial. It's clearly a necessity if you don't know the person's phone number.

# Way # 50

# Decide What

Once you've settled on your approach, you'll have to decide on an appropriate activity for your first date. A party is a good idea. It's relaxed, it gives the impression that you lead an active social life, and it eliminates the need for keeping up a constant one-on-one conversation. Downside: The party could be a genuine disaster, your first date is open to public scrutiny, and—worst of all—the prospective lover could fall for a fellow guest. Try this: Consider hosting your own party. Then you can handpick the guests and show off your social skills on your home turf.

If you don't go for the security-in-numbers gambit or the date is a relative stranger, meet at a bar or restaurant.

Whatever you plan, keep it relatively inexpensive. Not cheap, but reasonable. The one who does the asking—that's you, baby—should reach for the check first. If your date offers to pay, it's your call. Even today, most guys don't automatically assume that a woman will pay.

# Just Ask

The next step is the big one. Take a deep breath and ask away. Don't say, "Would you like to get together sometime?" "Sometime" has a way of becoming "never." If you really want a date, try, "Would you like to go to [name of event] with me at [exact time] on Saturday?"

# Way # 50

OK, now you've met the love of your life, you made all the right moves, and your relationship flourished. But here it is a few months later and the bloom is off the rose. How can you get out of a relationship that's gone wrong? Just turn this book over and see.

**H** ere are a few more tried-and-true breakup lines you can use. All have been field-tested by our team of experts. They report excellent results:

**Choice 1:** "Let's just be friends."

**Choice 2:** "I'm not ready for a relation-ship."

**Choice 3:** "It's getting too serious too fast."

All these approaches allow the soon-to-be-ex to escape graciously. But if these aren't your style, how about . . .

**way #3**

**some lovely lies**

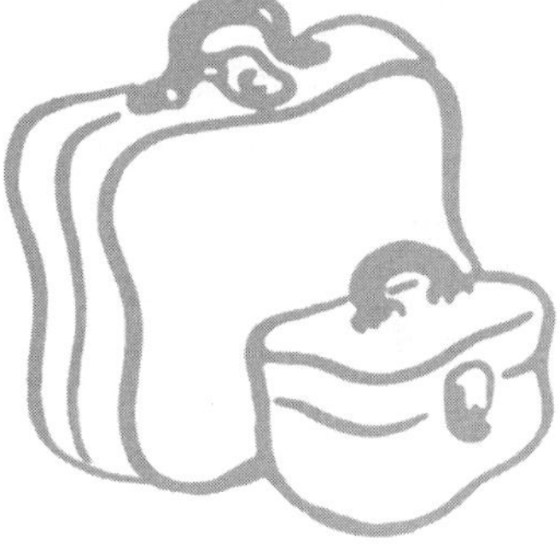

**50 WAYS TO DROP YOUR LOVER**

4

**A**nother nice way to break off a relationship is to plead future commitments. Try these methods:

**Opening line:** "I would love to continue this relationship, but I'm not allowed to get serious with a person until . . .

**Choice A:** I finish my Ph.D. [M.D., etc.]."

**Choice B:** I'm 25 years old [insert appropriate age]."

**Choice C:** My older sister gets married."

**Choice D:** I've been working for at least a decade."

**Choice E:** I qualify for the Olympics."

way #4

back to the future

**Choice F:** I win the lottery."

**Note:** *This approach works equally well if you want to brush off a request for a date. Consider: "I would love to go out with you but I can't date until I master at least three foreign languages."*

You know you can't move on until you unpack your emotional luggage. (That's a 90s way of saying, "You can't date anyone else until you get this lug/lugette off your mind.") So use this as an opportunity to complete a relationship powerfully.

Sit down with your lover and say . . .

**Choice 1:** "I feel confused."

**Choice 2:** "I don't know what I want any-more."

**Choice 3:** "I know I'm emotionally involved with you, but I don't know if it's love. So I think it's best if we end our relationship now."

# way #5

# ditch the
# emotional
# baggage

# way #6

## the selfless approach

**A**re you the self-sacrificing sort? Do people envision you skipping across the ice floes to rescue a lost gerbil or patiently standing in line during the holiday season to buy the perfect set of highball glasses for Aunt Ethel? Do you often pack extra drinks in case anyone gets thirsty or carry a quarter tucked into your shoe for an emergency phone call?

If this description fits you, consider using the following dialogue when you decide to leave your lover:

**Choice 1:** "I feel I'm just holding you back."

**Choice 2:** "You need to be free to pursue your dream."

**Choice 3:** "I wish it didn't have to be this way."

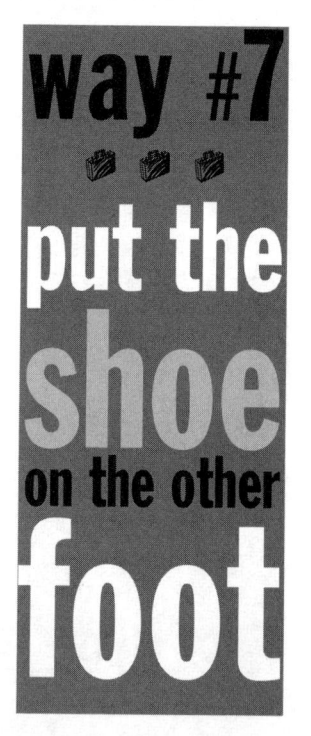

If the gentle kiss-offs are too subtle, it's time to move to Stage 2: Intentionally Annoying Behavior. With this strategy, you intentionally get your lover to dislike you. In fact, if you're really clever about it, you can even make your lover take the final action. Try these tactics:

1. Be late for a very important evening. If you're the driver, pull up 30 minutes behind schedule. If you're the passenger, stall while getting ready.

2. If you're cohabitating, don't do anything constructive around the house. Stick to annoying pastimes. Leave glasses on the coffee table or towels on the floor, hog the bathroom in the morning, or leave the lights on late into the night—whatever is most likely to irritate your live-in partner.

3. In public, make a point of noticing attractive specimens of the opposite sex. Make it good and obvious that you're on the prowl: Get some swivel into that head motion.

**way #7**

**put the shoe on the other foot**

## way #8

## add a little fuel to the fire

When your beloved complains about your behavior, act much put-upon. Sigh with great angst and say something like, "Get off my back. I'm not doing anything wrong. You think I'm perfect or something?"

To belabor the obvious, at some point in the process, throw in some zingers. These should be slightly derogatory and mean-spirited but not overtly hostile.

- Women, comments about his bald patch, spreading paunch, or inadequate paycheck work well.

- Men, try a swipe at the size of her posterior or the appearance of gray in her hair.

The comment should not be so mean as to be obvious. If it comes up in a later conversation, claim it was an unintentional blunder.

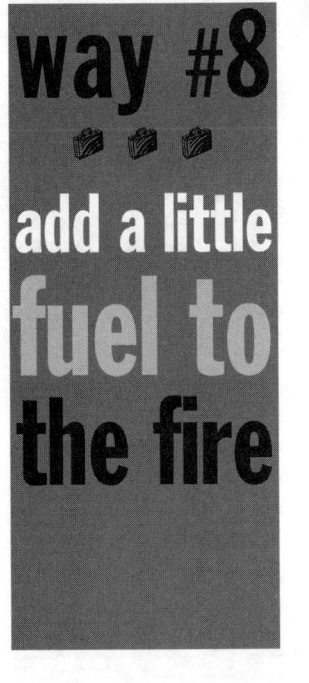

**S**eize these insults as an opportunity in disguise. Goad your lover into an argument to get your real feelings out in the open. Even better, try to maneuver him or her into taking the lead and starting the Big Breakup Fight.

The fight shouldn't be mean or bitter, but must accomplish the intended goal—ending the relationship. Viola! The deed is done and you're off the hook.

This method is not for the faint of heart—or for those who fight all the time anyway. One fight more or less won't signal your true intentions to your lover; he or she will just assume that it's more of the same thing . . . and a great make-up is in the future.

But what if all your provocation doesn't produce the big confrontation? What then? Read on . . .

**way #9**

**conflagration**

**!**

## way #10
## the
### phony-baloney
## war

This is one of the most beautiful breakup techniques of all: Trying to catch your lover in a mistake so he or she has an excuse to leave. That way, you're off the hook and guilt-free. For example, try declaring (for a fact, of course) that you know your lover is much taken with a coworker. Or, if your lover has to cancel plans, accuse him or her of "not being there for you."

The odds are good that your lover will insist that your charge is irrational (after all, it *is* irrational). With any luck, this will lead into a full-fledged argument. Soon, your lover should be firing off salvos of insults because he or she has been put in such a defensive position. You'll be firing your own insults in return. In other words, you've set up the perfect excuse for a breakup—and on your terms.

**C**orrections and criticism. You can't dump 'em faster and more effectively than by picking, picking, picking. This technique also has the advantage of making the other person think that he or she is getting the better end of the deal by wriggling free of such a nag.

If you're a woman, try, "Don't you know that's the wrong spoon for soup?" or "You call that kissing?" If you're a man, how about, "Do you really need that extra piece of cake?" or "Where did you get that awful haircut?"

No man wants to date his mother; no woman will stand for such carping. Be swift and you'll both suffer less.

**way #11**

**a lot of criticism goes a l-o-n-g way**

# way #12

## make it better by letter

If you can't bring yourself to say it, try writing a letter to end your relationship with a touch of class. "Snail mail" (the U.S. mail) buys you time before your lover finds out that the end has come.

If your lover didn't understand why you had to leave a relationship that seemed fine to him or her, here's your chance to explain it all, nicely and in sufficient detail—without any interruptions.

**WARNING: Write the letter and then let it sit. Give yourself a day or two to think about what you said. If you still agree with your wording and sentiments, send it off. If not, there's still a chance for revisions. Maybe you want to take out that line about her impossible mother or his uncouth best friend.**

14

**E**-mail (electronic mail) gives instant gratification and has that modern touch. If you're not especially skilled in grammar and spelling, e-mail might just be the ticket for you, because you can always explain away any errors as "bad typing."

Here are a few guidelines to consider if you decide to end your relationship via e-mail:

- Your significant other must also be online; otherwise, you're sending your e-mail off to the great web in the sky.

- Never, never, never e-mail to a third party and expect him/her to deliver the breakup e-mail to your lover.

- Never send a breakup e-mail to your lover's office or place of business.

- Even if you erase your e-mail, computer geniuses can recover it from a hard drive. As a

way #13

end it
instantly
with
e-mail

15

## 50 WAYS TO DROP YOUR LOVER

result, do your personal e-mail from home, never from the office. This is especially crucial if you are ending an office romance.

- Be especially careful when you send your e-mail. Press the wrong button and everyone on the planet will have a copy of your breakup letter.

**N**ot good with the written word? Not to worry; greeting cards to the rescue. When You Care Enough to Send the Very Best, try a breakup card.

The card can be snappy, sassy, or sappy. Pick the one that suits your style—and your feelings about your soon-to-be ex. Want to go out with a little élan? Consider springing for a super deluxe card. You know the kind . . . embossed cover, three or four pages long, lots of cute illustrations. Sick and tired of the relationship and just want to bolt? Pick a budget special with a corny message. Either way, you're just about off the hook. Add a line or two and you're scot-free.

**WARNING: Resist the urge to sign the card with the usual "love"!**

## way #14

# the
## hallmark
## of excellence

## way #15

## too much of a good thing

If you can't bring yourself to tell the truth, and the time-honored "it's not you it's me" speech doesn't work, try suffocation. Smother your soon-to-be-ex with attention.

Try calling 10, 20 times a day; insist on being together every night, every lunch, every weekend. You advance; he or she retreats. It's one of the basic laws of nature.

This method also has the advantage of convincing you that you made the right decision. You won't be tempted to waver once you spend *that* much time with the one you no longer love.

**C**an't dump 'em with a line or suffocation? Try wild emotionalism. This works best with women, but it's surprisingly effective with men, too. The more you weep and whine, the colder that lover will become. Just watch.

If you want to end the relationship in a hurry, try the wildly emotional approach in a public place. One good hysterical fit in a restaurant, bar, or at a concert will put the kibosh on that relationship posthaste.

**way #16**

**emotional overload**

## way #17

## woe is me

The self-pity speech is another effective lead-in to a brush-off. Try to get your soon-to-be-former lover to believe that you're confused—but that your confusion has nothing to do with your partner. That way, your lover will be more accepting down the road when you actually break it off. For example, you can book a nice dinner, wait until after dessert, then lean forward and say, "I'm not sure I like myself very much lately." Or, "I'm in a bad place with my career right now." Or, "I'm exploring my inner needs."

This is your lover's cue to nod sympathetically. Then you follow with, "I sometimes wonder how I can fulfill your needs when I can't even fulfill my own." Then comes the climax: "I just don't want to hurt you."

If your lover is the clever sort, he or she will interrupt this well-planned denouement at the point where you say, "You deserve better," with "You're right. I do deserve better." Then your lover will exit gleefully. Either way, you've accomplished your goal.

20

This sounds like common sense, and it is. But common sense, like a cheerful clerk at the Department of Motor Vehicles, is in short supply nowadays. Remember what your mama always said: "You can't have your cake and eat it, too." Well, you can't break up and continue to date your former lover, either. It's got to be one or the other.

So let's assume that you finally pulled the plug on this relationship. It's over, kaput, finito. Even if you and your ex broke up with civility, don't think that you can just shift into friendship mode.

If you want a final break, change your habits. Rule out all opportunities for chance meetings. Take a different train, subway, or bus. Change your lunch hour and place; find a new coffee bar. Nix on the same newspaper stand. Keep yourself away from your ex so you can clear your head and decide what you want.

**way #18**

**stop all dates**

## way #19

$$E = MC^2$$

Try a little physics, à la Uncle Albert's theory of space and time. Here are two gentle but effective breakup lines you can use if they suit your style:

TIME            "I need a little time to sort out my feelings."

SPACE           "I need some space."

Not nuclear enough? Go on to . . .

**W**ith everyone's sexuality changing so fast nowadays, a sexual breakup approach can be both creative and plausible.

First, try this sentence:

*"I'm exploring my sexuality, so we have to part ways."*

If that doesn't work, move on to:

*"I've discovered I'm gay (a lesbian)."*

Obviously, whatever you pick as your sexual orientation for the purposes of this exercise cannot be that which your lover might find attractive.

Finally, if you're gay or a lesbian, try:

*"I've discovered that I'm straight."*

## way #20

## sexual

## ploys

# way #21

## stand up and take the blame

Try the following speech if you want to break up your relationship with some elegance:

*"It's not you; it's me. I've changed. I need something different now, and you shouldn't have to change to suit me, because you're perfect just the way you are. But I have to leave. So this is good-bye."*

Then leave, quietly.

**Note:** *If you're in a bar or restaurant, pay the bill before you exit. It's a nice touch . . . and you never know what the future will bring. The person you're leaving could end up being your boss.*

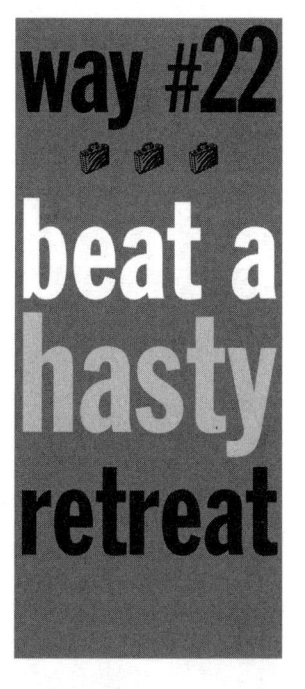

If things are not going well with the breakup ploys, you can always just run for cover. Try these surefire exit lines (and don't look back):

1. (Look out the window.) "Oh no! My car's being towed away."

2. "Would you excuse me? I really need to find a bathroom."

3. (Clutch your eye.) "My contact lens!"

4. "Oops, I have to take my medication right now, or else . . . ."

**way #22**

**beat a hasty retreat**

## way #23

### get a little help from above

Seeking divine intervention is another approach to ending a bad relationship. No, that doesn't mean praying for your partner to be struck by lightning or carried off by a giant bird of prey. It means a real change of heart.

To whit:

**Male exit line:** "I feel a call to the priesthood."

**Female exit line:** "I've decided to become a bride of Christ."

**Note:** *This works best if you're of the Catholic persuasion.*

**S**o far, we haven't considered the depth of the relationship and the time that you've invested into it. If you've only been dating a few weeks and you haven't been sexually intimate, your breakup can be short and hopefully sweet. But if you've been going out for months or (Heaven forbid) years, you are very likely going to get stuck spending a lot of time discussing the breakup with your partner. There will be a lot of hashing out of details, deciding who gets the Hootie CD you bought together, and arguing over the fate of the once-scrawny stray dog that followed you home and stayed.

This is not a time to stint. Invest the time you need to break off the relationship neatly and cleanly. Resign yourself to the fact that you may have to spend hours or even days making the break.

**way #24**

**the time factor**

# way #25

## the neutral zone

If you're severing a l-o-n-g relationship, be sure to meet on neutral territory each and every time. Stay out of your house, your partner's house, or the house you shared. Meeting in the Neutral Zone gives a different tone to the meetings and reduces the likelihood that you're going to get romantic and further delay the inevitable end.

Try to choose a place where you are not likely to run into friends. Here are some good possibilities to consider:

- A new restaurant
- An unfamiliar coffee bar
- A bar in another part of town
- A park
- A beach

If you're a person who likes to be precise, try this exchange when ending a relationship:

**You:** "How do you know when you're in love?"

**Partner:** [Provides definition]

**You:** "That's not how I feel about you. I guess we should break up."

This has the advantage of placing the burden on your partner and leaving you to cut the cord fast.

**way #26**

**go by the book**

## way #27

## change your phone number

This may be a cowardly way out, but sometimes it's the only way to go. If it's impossible to talk to your lover about breaking up or if you talk and talk without ever getting through, you may have to resort to a permanent disconnect.

Remember, however, that it's not enough to simply change your telephone number. Unless you request an unlisted number, you'll find yourself right back where the relationship started.

In extreme cases, you might also want to change your fax number and e-mail address, too.

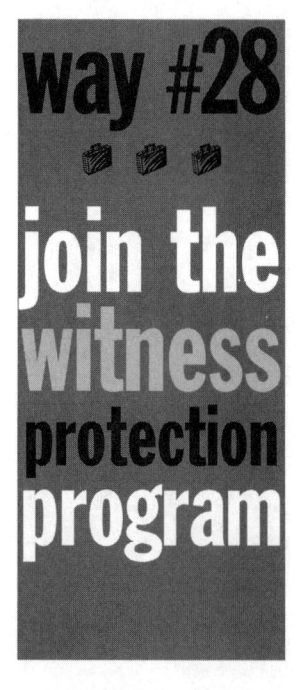

OK, it's a little extreme, but we hear that South Dakota is very nice at this time of the year. Seriously, there are times when all the dialogue in the world doesn't accomplish your aim. There are some lovers who just won't take "no" for an answer.

If you find yourself in this situation, it may be time to fold your tent and leave town. People can do awfully odd things when they have been thwarted in love. You don't have to stick around to find out.

**way #28**

**join the witness protection program**

## way #29

## thanks for the memories

When in doubt, fall back on good manners. You can't go wrong being polite and genuinely honest and decent when you end a relationship.

Start by telling your partner that the relationship isn't working for you and that you're not willing to make the necessary changes to make it work. As a result, you want to end the relationship.

Then thank your partner for the time and energy he or she put into the relationship. Be sincere with your thanks. Stick to real things. Even the worst relationships have something you can be thankful for . . . perhaps it's just the time invested or that terrific recipe for shrimp scampi.

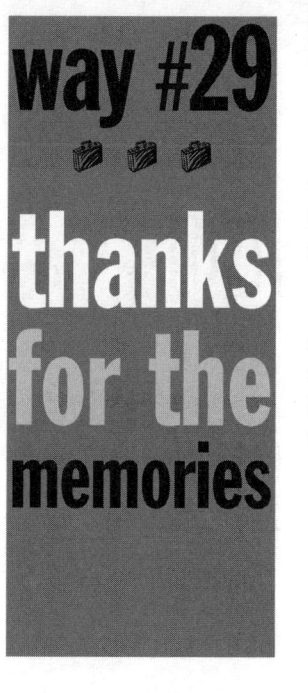

**A** long with giving thanks when you break up a relationship, this is a good time to apologize for anything that you have done—or failed to do—that may have hurt your partner. Again, be genuine in your apology.

You may wish to think this through before you initiate the breakup. Preplanning can help you be precise as well as sincere. Allow your partner time to respond to your apologies. Let your partner voice his or her feelings about the breakup.

This could take a few minutes or a few hours, depending on how long you have been together.

Be polite and sincere.

**way #30**

**mea culpa***

*Latin for "It's all my fault."

# 50 WAYS TO DROP YOUR LOVER

**CAUTION:** If your partner gets abusive, get out. You never have to put up with nastiness, no matter how well-mannered you want to be.

When it's over, it's over. Avoid the impulse to ask for friendship. Often the person who initiates the breakup will end the discussion with a line like this: "I'd still like to be your friend" or "I hope we can still be friends" or "I'll always cherish your friendship." No.

Why do people say things like this when ending a relationship? They want to minimize the loss, both for themselves and their partners. They also mistakenly think that this softens the rejection.

In reality, if you're giving your partner the boot, chances are good that your partner is so deeply hurt that the last thing he or she wants is to stay your best buddy. Asking for friendship at a time like this is adding insult to injury.

If you are really destined to remain friends, the friendship will develop over time, without strain. Such a rap-

**way #31**

**best buddies**

prochement can take place only when your former lover feels comfortable enough to be with you again. It's definitely not something that should or will occur naturally at the end of a romance.

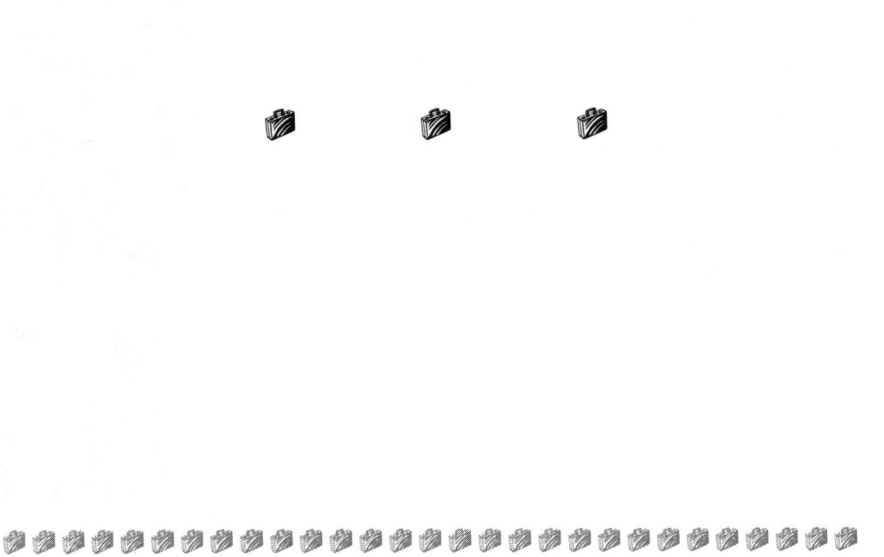

Like heavy lifting and macramé, breaking up is hard to do. As a result, the end of a relationship is an ideal time to take that long-overdue cruise, safari, or junket. Most people work too hard, anyway. Treat yourself to a nice vacation and give your breakup time to cool off at the same time.

By the time you get back, both you and your ex-lover will be in a different frame of mind. You'll find that it's easier to move on once you've had some long-distance breathing space.

**way #32**

**the expatriate route: leave the country**

## way #33

### when you hear the beep . . .

Can't do it face-to-face? Can't even do it live phone-to-phone? Try leaving a message on your ex-lover's answering machine. That way you don't have to actually talk to anyone and you won't be sidetracked.

This method works best if:

a. the relationship has been short.

b. you do not work together.

c. most of your communication was by phone and answering machine.

d. you live in different states.

e. you have a great speaking voice.

Then use your answering machine to screen all your messages for the next few weeks.

**G**.K. Chesterton once said, "Art, like morality, consists of drawing the line somewhere." And here's where you draw the line. Consider using an appeal to art and beauty when you make the break:

**Breakup line:** "I just can't picture us together."

**Follow up with:** "You're so attractive. You're bound to meet other people."

**way #34**

**beauty and the beast**

## way #35

## just the fax, Ma'am

**T**echnology is a wonderful thing, especially when you're getting ready to break up a relationship. For just a few dollars, you can send a breakup fax. There are several advantages to this method:

1.  Writing a fax gives you time to think out what you want to say. You can choose your words with care and be as gentle (or as cruel) as you want.

2.  Unlike a letter, a fax transmits instantly. Once you send it, it's gone and you're done with the relationship.

3.  Unlike e-mail, a fax cannot be retrieved from a disk. There are only two copies: yours and your ex's.

**Way # 35**

**Note:** *Never send a breakup fax to a person's place of employment (unless he or she works at home). Tacky, tacky, tacky.*

## way #36

## ding, dong

**S**ay it with flowers or FedEx. Consider stuffed animals or a courier service. Nothing like a home delivery to leave a good impression when you are ending a relationship. This works best with a brief relationship; a long-term affair warrants a more personalized leave-taking.

Write a brief message ending the relationship and tuck it into a bouquet, under the arm of a stuffed animal, or inside a FedEx mailer. Enclose your ex's apartment key, too.

**A** s a last resort, you can try this gambit:

*"I've taken a job in another city, so this is goodbye."*

The main problem, however, is that to make this work you really have to move to another city . . . preferably somewhere like Bora-Bora that doesn't get two FedEx shipments a day.

**way #37**

**exploring other options**

## way #38

## the ego boost

If you want to leave your lover feeling good, try an ego boost breakup. Here's a possibility that's worked well for a number of people:

**Male line:** "You're too much of a woman for me."

**Female line:** "You're too much of a man for me."

Hey, it may even be true.

**W**e all reach low points in our lives, but this excuse really hits rock bottom:

*"I don't have too long to live and I don't want to spend that time with you."*

Of course, all's fair in love and breaking up. So use this line if it works for you and your particular love affair.

way #39

try not to sink this low . . .

## way #40

## leave already

Here's another seemingly commonsense tactic. Say what you have to say and beat a hasty retreat. Interestingly, this is often the most difficult part of breaking up. Often the breakup conversation is the most honest exchange you have ever had with your lover, and that can spark unexpected feelings of intimacy. It is tempting to want to stay connected and so prolong those good feelings. It is not a good idea—unless you genuinely have second thoughts about the breakup.

Sometimes the honesty that takes place during a breakup actually does clear the path for something new to happen. If you both feel that way, it might be appropriate to try again. If there is any doubt at all, break contact and move on.

**H**aving second thoughts about breaking up? Try this sentence to leave the door open for a change of heart:

*"I'm not ready for a relationship right now."*

This implies that you may be in the mood for a relationship at some unspecified time in the future. And you never know: You may be . . .

way #41

foot
in the
door

## way #42

### a matter of timing

**D**eciding *when* to break up can be just as important as deciding *how* to break up, so choose your timing well.

Keep this chart in mind as you plan for the big event.

**OK**

Friday night
(Leaves weekend
for recovery)

**Not a Good Idea**

Your partner's birthday
(As if birthdays aren't bad
enough)

**Way # 42**

## OK

Tuesday
*(Lost day anyway)*

Dinner time
*(Leaves evening to recover)*

Evenings

## Not a Good Idea

Any major holiday: Christmas, etc.
*(This is my gift?)*

Lunch time
*(Does anyone want to return to the office after a breakup?)*

The anniversary of your first date

## way #43

### voyage to nowhere

Ever take a cruise to nowhere? You board the boat and sail around the harbor for a few hours. Too many people get caught in similar relationships. They sail around and around in circles. Break the cycle with these lines:

**You:** "Where do you think this relationship is heading?"

**Partner:** [Response]

**You:** "Well, I don't want to go there."

Then leave.

**S**ometimes you just have to think of yourself. Try one of these three sentences to extricate yourself from an unsatisfying relationship:

**Choice 1:** "It's not working for me."

**Choice 2:** "I'm going through a very selfish period and I have to think of me."

**Choice 3:** "I'm doing this as much for you as for me."

way #44

me, myself, and I

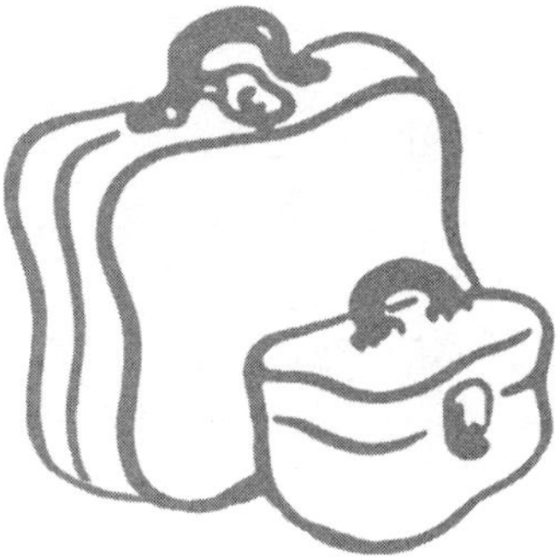

**50 WAYS TO DROP YOUR LOVER**

L ike most children, my daughter is disarmingly frank. When she has had enough of one of her friends, she says, "You're driving me crazy. I want you to go home now." Blunt and to the point. No one has ever misunderstood her message.

If your lover is obtuse or determined to resist the breakup, don't mince words. Say it flat out. Here are three more variations to try:

**Choice 1:** "I've met someone else, so this is good-bye."

**Choice 2:** "I'd like my key back."

**Choice 3:** "Our relationship is starting to remind me of my parents' relationship."

**way #45**

**about as subtle as a polo mallet to the side of the head**

## way #46
## friends

What are friends for? For one thing, they're for helping you get out of a bad relationship. If you can't phone, fax, FedEx, or e-mail to end a dead-end relationship, you can always get a friend to deliver the news. This may take some bribery ("I'll treat you to a great dinner") or begging ("I won't ever ask for another favor"), but it's worth it if it gets you off the hook.

The best idea, of course, is to see if your friend would like to date your ex—then you've done your good deed for the day as well.

**F**or you pet lovers out there, you can always pin the breakup on your beloved creatures. Try this simple approach:

*"My cat (dog, ferret, iguana) doesn't like you."*

**CAUTION: You really must have a current, live pet for this method to work. And your lover should have been attacked by the pet at least once.**

## way #47

# man's
## (and woman's)
# best
# friend

## way #48

## save yourself

If your relationship has been emotionally or physically abusive, you have no obligation at all to discuss your reasons for leaving. Just make a beeline for the door and go. Remember *The Invasion of the Body Snatchers*: "Save yourself." Trying to explain yourself to an abusive partner will not get you anywhere. In fact, it will make you more vulnerable to false promises of change or other forms of manipulation.

Say, "It's over," and leave.

Since these are often very difficult relationships to end, you might want to speak to a health care professional to help you get over the rough patches.

**C**an't bring yourself to take that final step, even after all you've just read? OK, how about a "trial separation"? With any luck, the breakup will last several months, though more often than not it only lasts one sodden weekend. If you're a guy, you'll think a lot and drink too much beer and wake up with one hell of a headache. If you're a woman, you'll think a lot and have your nails done or clean the refrigerator. You'll both feel stupid and shallow.

**DANGER: You may find yourself thinking (or heaven forbid saying) "Hey, my ex wasn't so bad. What am I looking for, the perfect man/woman (pick one)?"**

## way #49

## the
## trial
## separation

This is followed by a tearful reunion scene, some cold Chinese food, and each of you saying, "I'm sorry for the way I acted." You rent a movie, cuddle a little, and wind up saying: "We still need to work out some problems, but essentially everything is OK."

Time to move on to Way #50.

**W**hen you decide to leave your lover, really leave him or her. Don't drive past the house at 2:00 a.m. just to make sure he or she is alive. Don't call and say, "I just remembered I left some books at your place. When can I come to pick them up?" Don't seek out your ex-lover's best friend and probe for an update.

Chances are, this behavior shows that you're not ready to make the break. It ain't over 'till it's over, your subconscious is saying. Have that Last Talk and realize that it is time to go.

Then when you're ready to climb back on the emotional roller coaster, just turn this book over and read about 50 ways to meet a new lover.

way #50

no long good-byes

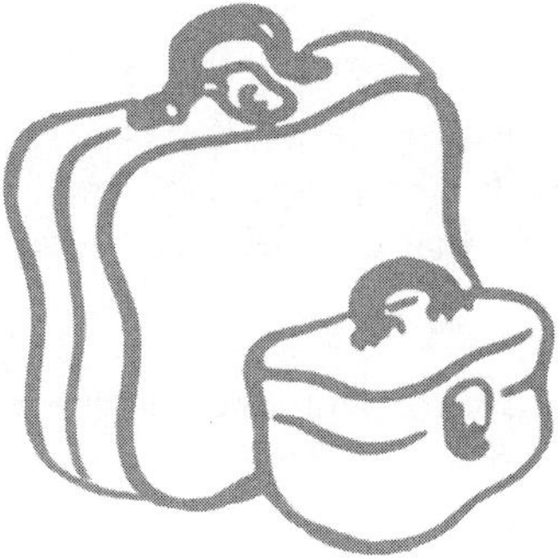

50 WAYS TO DROP YOUR LOVER